I have not stopped giving thanks for you,
remembering you in my prayers.

EPHESIANS 1:16

ZONDERVAN®

Prayers for a Woman's Soul
Copyright © 2005 by Zondervan

Requests for information should be addressed to:

Zondervan, *Grand Rapids, Michigan 49530*

ISBN-13: 978-0-310-81181-7

Interior design by Christopher Gilbert & Robin Black, UDG DesignWorks

Printed in China

08 09 10 11 12 • 14 13 12 11 10 9 8 7 6 5 4 3

Prayers
FOR
A Woman's
SOUL

ZONDERVAN®

Our prayer and God's mercy

are like two buckets in a well; while the

one ascends the other descends.

MARK HOPKINS

Susanna Wesley, mother of nineteen children including the great clergymen John and Charles Wesley, was said to throw her apron over her head in order to spend a few precious moments in prayer. You may not have nineteen children, or nine, or even one. But you almost certainly know how difficult it is to find time to pray in our high-speed world.

And yet, prayer is something that no thoughtful woman dare do without. It is both the tether that will keep her safely grounded and the kite that will allow her to rise above her circumstances and glimpse eternity. Prayer is a remedy for worry in a world with so much to worry about, and it is a hope magnifier in those times when worry takes on the face of reality. Still, prayer has a higher purpose and a greater reward than these that have been mentioned. Prayer, even in its simplest and most unpretentious form, is personal conversation with the loving and benevolent Creator of the universe.

Prayers for a Woman's Soul touches on the many aspects of prayer. We've included high prayers and everyday prayers—prayers that flow effortlessly from the abundance of a thankful heart and prayers that are carefully crafted to embody noble pursuits. We hope that as you read through these pages, you will be inspired to spend time talking to that special Someone who has been carefully listening for your voice—God himself.

The wings of prayer carry high and far.

CONTENTS

Prayers
OF *love*
AND *Trust*

Lord, help me to be patient and kind toward others. Help me not to boast when I'm right or be proud when others are wrong. Help me not to be rude. I don't want my love to be self-seeking, or easily angered. And, Lord, convict me if I start keeping a record of wrongs, for I desire that my love will always rejoice with the truth. Help me to have faith, hope, and love ever increasing, ever growing.

JONI EARECKSON TADA

Love is patient, love is kind. It does not envy,
it does not boast, it is not proud.
It is not rude, it is not self-seeking, it is not
easily angered, it keeps no record of wrongs.
Love does not delight in evil but rejoices
with the truth. It always protects,
always trusts, always hopes, always perseveres.
Love never fails.

1 CORINTHIANS 13:4–8

Love must be sincere. Hate what is evil;
cling to what is good.
Be devoted to one another in brotherly love.
Honor one another above yourselves.

ROMANS 12:9–10

He who covers over an offense promotes love.

PROVERBS 17:9

You yourselves have been taught
by God to love each other.

1 THESSALONIANS 4:9–10

These three remain: faith, hope and love.
But the greatest of these is love.

1 CORINTHIANS 13:13

Lord Jesus, grant me the trusting heart of a child that I might come into your presence and simply accept the gift of love already given. Fill me with your Holy Spirit, O Lord, that I might become like a shining light of truth in this dark world. I am weak, Lord, and often fail. But, oh, what glory it is to be able to talk with you, to know you are near, that you care. I love you, Lord, with all my heart. Amen.

ROSALIND RINKER

Those who know your name will trust in you,
for you, LORD, have never forsaken
those who seek you.

PSALM 9:10

Surely God is my salvation;
I will trust and not be afraid.
The LORD, the LORD, is my strength and my song;
he has become my salvation.

ISAIAH 12:2

Prayer to a heart of lowly love
Opens the gate of heaven above.
Ah, prayer is God's high dwelling-place,
Wherein His children see His face.
From earth to heaven we build a stair:
The name by which we call it—prayer.
Love's rain, the Spirit's holy ray,
And tears of joy, are theirs who pray.

NARAYAN VAMAN TILAK

(TRANS. NICOL MACNICOLL)

Prayer is an expression of our relationship with God. If we are to grow spiritually, we must be honest. God knows the stuff we are made of—and he loves us anyway! He loves us more than anything we can imagine. And even more than any loving father is prepared to deal with the questions and complaints of his children, God is prepared to listen to us. He wants us to know him, to trust him, and to come to a closer understanding of his ways. He wants our love. Above all, God wants to give us the answer we are looking for—the answer that only he can give.

MARCIA HOLLIS

I call on you, O God, for you will answer me;
give ear to me and hear my prayer.

PSALM 17:6

Praise be to God,
who has not rejected my prayer
or withheld his love from me!

PSALM 66:20

*Jesus said, "My prayer is not for them alone.
I pray also for those who will believe in me
through their message, that all of them may be
one, Father, just as you are in me and I am in
you. May they also be in us so that the world
may believe that you have sent me. I have given
them the glory that you gave me, that they may
be one as we are one: I in them and you in me.
May they be brought to complete unity to let the
world know that you sent me and have loved
them even as you have loved me. Father, I want
those you have given me to be with me where
I am, and to see my glory, the glory you have
given me because you loved me before the
creation of the world."*

JOHN 17:20–24

PRAYER IS THE SOUL'S SINCERE DESIRE

Prayer is the soul's sincere desire,
unuttered or expressed,
the motion of a hidden fire
that trembles in the breast.
Prayer is the burden of a sigh,
the falling of a tear,
the upward glancing of an eye,
when none but God is near.
Prayer is the simplest form of speech
that infant lips can try;
prayer the sublimest strains that reach
the Majesty on high.

Prayer is the contrite sinners' voice,
      returning from their way,
      while angels in their songs rejoice
      and cry, "Behold, they pray!"
Prayer is the Christians' vital breath,
      the Christians' native air;
      their watchword at the gates of death;
      they enter heaven with prayer.
O thou, by whom we come to God,
      the Life, the Truth, the Way:
      the path of prayer thyself hast trod;
      Lord, teach us how to pray!

JAMES MONTGOMERY

Lord Jesus, remind me continually that your love seeks nothing for itself but gives generously out of its abundance. Because you love me, I always have love to give away to anyone who crosses my path. Let me experience the joy of giving in your name. Amen.

BARBARA JOHNSON

Jesus said, "A new command I give you:
Love one another. As I have loved you,
so you must love one another.
By this all men will know that you are my
disciples, if you love one another."

JOHN 13:34-35

Dear friends, let us love one another,
for love comes from God. Everyone who loves
has been born of God and knows God.

1 JOHN 4:7

Jesus said, "I tell you: Love your enemies and
pray for those who persecute you."

MATTHEW 5:44

We love because he first loved us.

1 JOHN 4:19

"'Love the Lord your God with all your heart
and with all your soul and
with all your strength and with all your mind';
and, 'Love your neighbor as yourself.'"

LUKE 10:27

Lord God, where would I be without your love—a love that not only shelters me in the height of the storm but helps me grow and thrive no matter the weather. Each morning, I commit my way to you and entrust myself to your care.

REBECCA CURRINGTON

The Lord is good,
   a refuge in times of trouble.
He cares for those who trust in him.

NAHUM 1:7

I am like an olive tree
   flourishing in the house of God;
I trust in God's unfailing love
   for ever and ever.

PSALM 52:8

God is our refuge and strength,
an ever-present help in trouble.

PSALM 46:1

Your love, O LORD, reaches to the heavens,
your faithfulness to the skies.
Your righteousness is like the mighty mountains,
your justice like the great deep.
O LORD,, you preserve both man and beast.
How priceless is your unfailing love!
Both high and low among men
find refuge in the shadow of your wings.

PSALM 36:5–7

Lord Jesus, I am who I am by your loving design. Help me to accept my weaknesses as well as my strengths. Help me, too, to embrace myself in my totality as you embrace me, knowing I cannot do what was not ordained for me. May I contentedly serve you, love you, and luxuriate in what you empower me to do in your name and for your sake. Amen.

MARILYN MEBERG

We are God's workmanship,
created in Christ Jesus to do good works,
which God prepared in advance for us to do.

EPHESIANS 2:10

You created my inmost being;
  you knit me together in my mother's womb.
I praise you because I am fearfully and
      wonderfully made;
  your works are wonderful,
  I know that full well.
My frame was not hidden from you
    when I was made in the secret place.
When I was woven together in the depths
      of the earth,
  your eyes saw my unformed body.
All the days ordained for me
    were written in your book
    before one of them came to be.

PSALM 139:13–16

Lord, I want to bless you with praise for your gift of forgiveness given through the death and resurrection of your Son, Jesus Christ. Your marvelous love has set me free from the guilt and consequences of my sin. Because you are loving, you are forgiving. I rejoice and am humbled by your abundant forgiveness.

FERN NICHOLS

In Christ we have redemption
through his blood, the forgiveness of sins,
in accordance with the riches of God's grace.

EPHESIANS 1:7

The Lord our God is merciful and forgiving,
even though we have rebelled against him.

DANIEL 9:9

*It was not with perishable things such as silver
or gold that you were redeemed from the
empty way of life handed down to you from your
forefathers, but with the precious
blood of Christ, a lamb without blemish or defect.*

1 PETER 1:18–19

*Put your hope in the LORD,
for with the Lord is unfailing love
and with him is full redemption.*

PSALM 130:7

*When the kindness and love of
God our Savior appeared, he saved us, not
because of righteous things we had done,
but because of his mercy. He saved us through
the washing of rebirth and renewal by
the Holy Spirit, whom he poured out on us
generously through Jesus Christ our Savior,
so that, having been justified by his grace,
we might become heirs having
the hope of eternal life.*

TITUS 3:4–7

Prayer is my link to sanity, stability, and longevity.

Am I suggesting we live longer when we pray? Possibly. There's nothing like quiet reflective moments to encourage our blood pressures to stop percolating, our hearts to fall back into rhythm, and our minds to stop gyrating. Then add to all of that the untold benefits of loving exchanges with our all-knowing, all-seeing, all-powerful God. He who assigns our days and redeems our losses has a way of calming our anxieties and even healing our infirmities.

I love that the Lord is not only hospitable but he is also invitational. That's probably why he is said to be "The Door." Jesus makes our entrance to the Father possible. He knew we would need time in his presence, time when we can step out of the whirlwind and into his consoling company. It is there, as we lean our heads upon his breast, that we are both deeply heard and deeply understood.

PATSY CLAIRMONT

*Jesus says to you, "Ask and it will be given
to you; seek and you will find; knock and the door
will be opened to you. For everyone who
asks receives; he who seeks finds; and to him
who knocks, the door will be opened."*

LUKE 11:9–10

*Jesus said, "Ask and it will be given to you;
seek and you will find; knock and the door will
be opened to you. For everyone who
asks receives; he who seeks finds; and to him
who knocks, the door will be opened.
Which of you, if his son asks for bread, will give
him a stone? Or if he asks for a fish,
will give him a snake? If you, then, though you
are evil, know how to give good gifts
to your children, how much more will your
Father in heaven give good gifts
to those who ask him!"*

MATTHEW 7:7–11

Prayer is the expression of a human heart in conversation with God. The more natural the prayer, the more real he becomes. It has all been simplified for me to this extent. Prayer is a dialogue between two persons who love each other.

ROSALIND RINKER

*The LORD would speak to Moses
face to face, as a man speaks with his friend.*

EXODUS 33:11

*You will call upon me and come
and pray to me, and I will listen to you.*

JEREMIAH 29:12

One day Jesus was praying in a certain place.
When he finished, one of his disciples
said to him, "Lord, teach us
to pray, just as John taught his disciples."
He said to them, "When you pray, say:

"'Father,
hallowed be your name,
your kingdom come.
Give us each day our daily bread.
Forgive us our sins,
for we also forgive everyone who sins
against us.
And lead us not into temptation.'"

LUKE 11:1–4

Lord, I need to confess that I haven't always trusted in you with all my heart. Forgive me for leaning on my own understanding when the road gets rough. I acknowledge today that I am not promised an easy path, just a straight one, if I trust entirely in you. Lord, with every pothole, rut, or barrier I may come across, help me to remember to lean on you.

JONI EARECKSON TADA

God will not grow tired or weary,
and his understanding no one can fathom.
He gives strength to the weary
and increases the power of the weak.

ISAIAH 40:28−29

Trust in the LORD and do good;
  dwell in the land and enjoy safe pasture.
Delight yourself in the LORD
  and he will give you the desires of
    your heart.

PSALM 37:3–4

It is better to take refuge in the LORD
  than to trust in man.

PSALM 118:8

You will keep in perfect peace
  him whose mind is steadfast,
  because he trust in you.

ISAIAH 26:3

Father, in thy mysterious presence kneeling,
fain would our souls feel all thy
kindling love;
For we are weak, and need some deep revealing
of trust and strength and calmness
from above.

SAMUEL JOHNSON

You will find in your "closet of prayer" what you frequently lose when you are out in the world. The more you visit it, the more you will want to return. If you are faithful to your secret place, it will become your closest friend and bring you much comfort. The tears shed there bring cleansing.

THOMAS Á KEMPIS

The LORD has heard my cry for mercy;
the LORD accepts my prayer.

PSALM 6:9

May the God of hope fill you with all joy
and peace as you trust in him,
so that you may overflow with hope by the
power of the Holy Spirit.

ROMANS 15:13

The LORD your God is with you,
he is mighty to save.
He will take great delight in you,
he will quiet you with his love,
he will rejoice over you with singing.

ZEPHANIAH 3:17

Father, thank you that you can create something beautiful out of what appears to be dead. You do it every day. I'm grateful for your creative ideas that cost nothing but demonstrate your love for me. Amen.

LUCI SWINDOLL

The desert and the parched land will be glad;
*   the wilderness will rejoice and blossom.*
Like the crocus, it will burst into bloom;
*   it will rejoice greatly and shout for joy.*

ISAIAH 35:1-2

You, O LORD, have delivered my soul from death,
my eyes from tears,
my feet from stumbling,
that I may walk before the Lord
in the land of the living.

PSALM 116:8–9

If anyone is in Christ, he is a new creation;
the old has gone, the new has come!
All this is from God, who reconciled us to
himself through Christ.

2 CORINTHIANS 5:17–18

The LORD says, "I am doing a new thing!
Now it springs up; do you not perceive it?
I am making a way in the desert
and streams in the wasteland."

ISAIAH 43:18–19

Lord, what a risk you took loving us. Give us the wisdom and courage to risk loving you in return. Amen.

PATSY CLAIRMONT

God demonstrates his own love for us in this:
While we were still sinners, Christ died for us.

ROMANS 5:8

Love the LORD, all his saints!
The LORD preserves the faithful.

PSALM 31:23

Love the LORD your God, listen to his voice,
and hold fast to him. For the LORD is your life.

DEUTERONOMY 30:20

I will not doubt, though all my ships at sea
    come drifting home with broken masts
    and sails;
I shall believe the hand which never fails,
    from seeming evil worketh good to me.
And, though I weep because those sails are battered,
    still will I cry, while my best hopes
    lie shattered,
"I trust in thee."

ELLA WHEELER WILCOX

The salvation of the righteous comes
    from the LORD;
    he is their stronghold in time of trouble.

PSALM 37:39

Like art, like music, like so many other
disciplines, prayer can only be appreciated
when you actually spend time in it.
Spending time with the Master will elevate
your thinking. The more you pray, the more
will be revealed. You will understand. You
will smile and nod your head as you identify
with others who fight long battles and find
great joy on their knees.

JONI EARECKSON TADA

David said about the Lord,
"You have made known to me the paths of life;
you will fill me with joy in your presence."

ACTS 2:25, 28

Light is shed upon the righteous
and joy on the upright in heart.

PSALM 97:11

The eyes of the Lord are on the righteous and
his ears are attentive to their prayer.

1 P E T E R 3 : 1 2

Let everyone who is godly pray to you, LORD,
while you may be found;
surely when the mighty waters rise,
they will not reach him.

P S A L M 3 2 : 6

"Before they call I will answer;
while they are still speaking I will hear,"
says the LORD.

I S A I A H 6 5 : 2 4

Father, when my love grows thin, yours is abundant—for me, in me, and through me. And because your love is forbearing, I can likewise forbear. I can go on ... patiently. You never said it would be easy, but you did say it would be possible. Thank you for your precious promises. Thank you for your powerful Word. Thank you for your enabling Holy Spirit. Thank you for your patient love.

NANCY KENNEDY

Love is patient, love is kind.

1 CORINTHIANS 13:4

As servants of God we commend ourselves
in every way: in purity, understanding,
patience and kindness;
in the Holy Spirit and in sincere love.

2 CORINTHIANS 6:4, 6

*Imitate those who through faith and patience
inherit what has been promised.*

HEBREWS 6:12

*Bear with each other and forgive
whatever grievances you may have against one
another. Forgive as the Lord forgave you.*

COLOSSIANS 3:13

*Encourage the timid, help the weak,
be patient with everyone.*

1 THESSALONIANS 5:14

How can I tell of such love to me?
You made me in your image
*   and hold me in the palm of your hand,*
your cords of love, strong and fragile as silk
*   bind me and hold me.*
Rich cords, to family and friends,
*   music and laughter echoing in memories,*
*   light dancing on the water, hills rejoicing.*
Cords that found me hiding behind carefully
built walls and led me out,
*   love that heard my heart break and*
*   despair and rescued me,*
*   love that overcame my fears and doubts*
*   and released me.*
The questions and burdens I carry you take,
*   to leave my hands free—to hold you,*
*   and others*
*   free to follow your cords as they move and*
*   swirl in the breeze,*
*   free to be caught up in the dance*
*   of your love,*
*   finding myself in surrendering to you.*
How can I tell of such love? How can I give to
such love?
I am, here am I.

CATHERINE HOOPER

The LORD says, "I have engraved you on the palms of my hands;
   your walls are ever before me."

ISAIAH 49:16

I will sing of the LORD's great love forever;
   with my mouth I will make your faithfulness
      known through all generations.

PSALM 89:1

Father, let me hold thy hand and like a child
walk with thee down all my days, secure in
thy love and strength.

THOMAS À KEMPIS

On my bed I remember you;
I think of you through the watches
of the night.
Because you are my help,
I sing in the shadow of your wings.
My soul clings to you;
your right hand upholds me.

PSALM 63:6–8

He who fears the LORD has a secure fortress,
and for his children it will be a refuge.

PROVERBS 14:26

We who have fled to take hold
of the hope offered to us may be greatly
encouraged. We have this hope
as an anchor for the soul, firm and secure.

HEBREWS 6:18–19

May your hand be ready to help me,
for I have chosen your precepts.
I long for your salvation, O Lord,
and your law is my delight.
Let me live that I may praise you,
and may your laws sustain me.

PSALM 119:173–175

I will praise the LORD, who counsels me;
even at night my heart instructs me.
I have set the LORD always before me.
Because he is at my right hand, I will not
be shaken.
Therefore my heart is glad and my tongue rejoices;
my body also will rest secure.

PSALM 16:7–9

Prayers
FOR God's
Will

When you need to make decisions and
nobody on earth understands, call him up.
When your problems seem unbearable, call
him up. When you want to praise him and
show appreciation for his wonderful work in
your life, call him up. When you want to
communicate with Someone who wants to
communicate with you and who has all the
answers to your questions, call him up.

THELMA WELLS

I guide you in the way of wisdom
and lead you along straight paths.

PROVERBS 4:11

Whoever serves me must follow me; and where
I am, my servant also will be.
My Father will honor the one who serves me.

JOHN 12:26

"Praise be to the name of God for ever and ever;
wisdom and power are his.
He changes times and seasons;
he sets up kings and deposes them.
He gives wisdom to the wise
and knowledge to the discerning.
He reveals deep and hidden things;
he knows what lies in darkness,
and light dwells with him.
I thank and praise you, O God of my fathers:
You have given me wisdom and power."

DANIEL 2:20–23

When we speak with God, our power of addressing him, of holding communion with him, and listening to his still, small voice, depends on our will being one and the same with his.

FLORENCE NIGHTINGALE

O Lord, I am yours. Do what seems good in your sight, and give me complete resignation to your will.

DAVID LIVINGSTONE

May the will of God, the Father, the Son, and the Holy Spirit be done! Amen.

MARTIN LUTHER

Dearest Lord,
Teach me to be generous;
Teach me to serve you as you deserve;
To give and not to count the cost,
To fight and not to heed the wounds,
To toil and not to seek for rest,
To labour and not to seek reward,
Except to know that I do your will.

IGNATIUS LOYOLA

"I am the Lord's servant," Mary answered.
"May it be to me as you have said."

LUKE 1:38

Lord, I am yours, I was born for you;
    what is your will for me?
Let me be rich or beggared,
    exulting or lamenting,
    comforted or lonely;
    since I am yours, yours only,
    what is your will for me?

SAINT TERESA OF AVILA

You guide me with your counsel,
    and afterward you will take me into glory.

PSALM 73:24

Since you are my rock and my fortress,
    for the sake of your name lead and guide me.

PSALM 31:3

"My thoughts are not your thoughts,

     neither are your ways my ways,"

          declares the LORD.

"As the heavens are higher than the earth,

     so are my ways higher than your ways

     and my thoughts than your thoughts.

As the rain and the snow

     come down from heaven,

and do not return to it

     without watering the earth

and making it bud and flourish,

     so that it yields seed for the sower and

          bread for the eater,

so is my word that goes out from my mouth:

     It will not return to me empty,

but will accomplish what I desire

     and achieve the purpose for which I sent it."

ISAIAH 55:8–11

Lord, on my own, my strength is puny and my convictions waver—except when it comes to exercising my own will! But your Word says to trust in you with my whole heart, and "lean not" on my own understanding, and in everything I do, acknowledge you.

I know that if you lead me to do something, you will provide the necessary strength—even the strength to do something I really don't want to do. But I also know that when I lack the willingness and the conviction, you can and will change my heart.

I want to rise like the sun, in your strength, and shine for your glory. Because I know your goodness and your mercy, I offer myself to you as an act of worship.

NANCY KENNEDY

Trust in the LORD with all your heart
and lean not on your own understanding.

PROVERBS 3:5

It is God who works in you to will and to act
according to his good purpose.

PHILIPPIANS 2:13

In view of God's mercy ... offer your bodies as
living sacrifices, holy and pleasing to God—this
is your spiritual act of worship. Do not conform
any longer to the pattern of this world, but be
transformed by the renewing of your mind. Then
you will be able to test and approve what God's
will is—his good, pleasing and perfect will.

ROMANS 12:1–2

Most high and glorious God, come and
enlighten the darkness of my heart. Give me
right faith, certain hope, and perfect love
that everything I do may be in fulfillment of
your holy will; through Jesus Christ my Lord.

SAINT FRANCIS OF ASSISI

Let the redeemed of the LORD say this—
God brought them out of darkness and the
deepest gloom
and broke away their chains.
Let them give thanks to the LORD for his
unfailing love.

PSALM 107:2, 14–15

Even in darkness light dawns for the upright,
for the gracious and compassionate and
righteous man.

PSALM 112:4

Who among you fears the LORD
and obeys the word of his servant?
Let him who walks in the dark,
who has no light,
trust in the name of the LORD
and rely on his God.

ISAIAH 50:10

The LORD says, "I will lead the blind by ways
they have not known,
along unfamiliar paths I will guide them;
I will turn the darkness into light before them
and make the rough places smooth.
These are the things I will do;
I will not forsake them."

ISAIAH 42:16

Give us a pure heart
that we may see thee.
A humble heart
that we may hear thee.
A heart of love
that we may serve thee.
A heart of faith
that we may live for thee.

DAG HAMMARSKJÖLD

Blessed are the pure in heart,
for they will see God.

MATTHEW 5:8

The LORD guides the humble in what is right
and teaches them his way.
All the ways of the LORD are loving and faithful.

PSALM 25:9–10

I glory in Christ Jesus in my service to God.

ROMANS 15:17

Jesus said, "I tell you the truth, anyone
who has faith in me will do what I have been
doing. He will do even greater things than these,
because I am going to the Father."

JOHN 14:12

Direct my footsteps according to your word;
let no sin rule over me.

PSALM 119:133

Grant me, O Lord, to know what is worth knowing, to love what is worth loving, to praise what delights you most, to value what is precious to you, and to reject whatever is evil in your eyes. Give me true discernment, so that I may judge rightly between things that differ. Above all, may I search out and do what is pleasing to you through Jesus Christ my Lord.

THOMAS À KEMPIS

Test everything. Hold on to the good.
Avoid every kind of evil.

1 THESSALONIANS 5:21–22

We have the mind of Christ.

1 CORINTHIANS 2:16

The discerning heart seeks knowledge.

PROVERBS 15:14

*Live as children of light (for the fruit of the
light consists in all goodness, righteousness and
truth) and find out what pleases the Lord.*

EPHESIANS 5:8–10

*I urge ... that requests, prayers, intercession
and thanksgiving be made for everyone—
for kings and all those in authority, that we may
live peaceful and quiet lives in all
godliness and holiness. This is good,
and pleases God our Savior.*

1 TIMOTHY 2:1–3

*Friends, if our hearts do not condemn us,
we have confidence before God and receive from
him anything we ask, because we obey
his commands and do what pleases him. And this
is his command: to believe in the name
of his Son, Jesus Christ, and to
love one another as he commanded us.*

1 JOHN 3:21–23

Dear Lord, forgive me for not trusting you
when I am in crisis. In those moments I find
myself feeling frustrated, angry, or scared,
I forget you are a good God and everything
you allow to happen in my life is for a purpose.
Forgive me for allowing my problems to
control my thoughts and actions instead of
trusting in your goodness for me.

FERN NICHOLS

*Consider it pure joy ... whenever you
face trials of many kinds, because you know that
the testing of your faith develops perseverance.
Perseverance must finish its work
so that you may be mature and complete,
not lacking anything.*

JAMES 1:2-4

*"Call upon me in the day of trouble;
I will deliver you, and you will honor me,"
declares the Lord.*

PSALM 50:15

Let everyone who is godly pray to you
          while you may be found;
surely when the mighty waters rise,
          they will not reach him.
You are my hiding place;
          you will protect me from trouble
          and surround me with songs of deliverance.

PSALM 32:6–7

Though you have made me see troubles,
          many and bitter,
          you will restore my life again;
from the depths of the earth
          you will again bring me up.
You will increase my honor
          and comfort me once again.

PSALM 71:20–21

Jesus, my Teacher, guide me along your way, and help me to piece together the jigsaw of life in your kingdom. When I make decisions, lead me to the heart of the matter, and when I face conflict, do not let my own panic drown out the still, small voice of your wisdom.

AUTHOR UNKNOWN

The LORD will guide you always;
*   he will satisfy your needs in a*
*   sun-scorched land*
*   and will strengthen your frame.*
You will be like a well-watered garden,
*   like a spring whose waters never fail.*

ISAIAH 58:11

Wisdom is sweet to your soul;
if you find it, there is a future hope for you,
and your hope will not be cut off.

PROVERBS 24:14

This is what the LORD *says:*
"Stand at the crossroads and look;
ask for the ancient paths,
ask where the good way is, and walk in it,
and you will find rest for your souls."

JEREMIAH 6:16

Commit your way to the LORD*;*
trust in him.

PSALM 37:5

God of our life, there are days when the burdens we carry chafe our shoulders and weigh us down; when the road seems dreary and endless, the skies grey and threatening; when our lives have no music in them, and our hearts are lonely, and our souls have lost their courage. Flood the path with light, we beseech thee; turn our eyes to where the skies are full of promise; tune our hearts to brave music; give us the sense of comradeship with heroes and saints of every age; and so quicken our spirits that we may be able to encourage the souls of all who journey with us on the road of life, to thy honor and glory.

SAINT AUGUSTINE OF HIPPO

Jesus said, "Come to me, all you who are weary and burdened, and I will give you rest. Take my yoke upon you and learn from me, for I am gentle and humble in heart, and you will find rest for your souls. For my yoke is easy and my burden is light."

MATTHEW 11:28–30

*Encourage one another daily, as long as
it is called Today, so that none of you may be
hardened by sin's deceitfulness.
Let us hold unswervingly to the hope we profess,
for he who promised is faithful.
And let us consider how we may spur one
another on toward love and good deeds.
Let us not give up meeting together, as some
are in the habit of doing, but let
us encourage one another—and all
the more as you see the Day approaching.*

HEBREWS 3:13; 10:23–25

*May our Lord Jesus Christ himself
and God our Father, who loved us and by his
grace gave us eternal encouragement and
good hope, encourage your hearts and strengthen
you in every good deed and word.*

2 THESSALONIANS 2:16–17

O Lord God, who called your servants to ventures of which we cannot see the ending, by paths as yet untrodden, through perils unknown: Give us faith to go out with a good courage, not knowing where we are going, but only that your hand is leading us, and your love supporting us; to the glory of your name.

Eric Milner-White & G.W. Griggs

If anyone serves, he should do it with the strength God provides, so that in all things God may be praised through Jesus Christ. To him be the glory and the power for ever and ever. Amen.

1 Peter 4:11

The LORD is my strength and my shield;
my heart trusts in him, and I am helped.

PSALM 28:7

It is God who arms me with strength
and makes my way perfect.

PSALM 18:32

Because the Sovereign LORD helps me,
I will not be disgraced.
Therefore have I set my face like flint,
and I know I will not be put to shame.

ISAIAH 50:7

O God, you are both the light and the guide of those who put their trust in you. Grant us in all our doubts and uncertainties the grace to ask what you would have us do; that the Spirit of wisdom may save us from all false choices, and that in your light we may see light; through Jesus Christ our Lord.

WILLIAM BRIGHT

Direct me in the path of your commands,
for there I find delight.
Turn my heart toward your statutes
and not toward selfish gain.
Turn my eyes away from worthless things;
preserve my life according to your word.

PSALM 119:35-37

Send forth your light and your truth,
let them guide me;
let them bring me to your holy mountain,
to the place where you dwell.
Then will I go to the altar of God,
to God, my joy and my delight.
I will praise you with the harp,
O God, my God.

PSALM 43:3–4

With you is the fountain of life;
in your light we see light.

PSALM 36:9

God, who said, "Let light shine
out of darkness," made his light shine in our
hearts to give us the light of the knowledge of
the glory of God in the face of Christ.

2 CORINTHIANS 4:6

My dearest Lord, be now a bright flame to
enlighten me, a guiding star to lead me,
a smooth path beneath my feet, and a
kindly shepherd along my way, today and
for evermore.

SAINT COLUMBIA

Jesus said, "When he, the Spirit of truth,
comes, he will guide you into all truth. He will
not speak on his own; he will
speak only what he hears, and he will tell
you what is yet to come."

JOHN 16:13

The Sovereign LORD tends his flock like a shepherd:
He gathers the lambs in his arms
and carries them close to his heart;
he gently leads those that have young.

ISAIAH 40:11

May the God of peace, who through
the blood of the eternal covenant brought back
from the dead our Lord Jesus, that great
Shepherd of the sheep, equip you with everything
good for doing his will, and may
he work in us what is pleasing to him,
through Jesus Christ, to whom be glory
for ever and ever. Amen.

HEBREWS 13:20–21

The LORD makes me lie down in
green pastures,
he leads me beside quiet waters,
he restores my soul.
He guides me in paths of righteousness
for his name's sake.

PSALM 23:2–3

The path of the righteous is level;
O upright One, you make the way of the
righteous smooth.

ISAIAH 26:7

Lord God, sanctify me—make me holy and prepare me for the work of your kingdom. I present myself to you without reservation to be used according to your eternal will and purpose.

ANDREA GARNEY

I desire to do your will, O my God;
your law is within my heart.

PSALM 40:8

Show me the way I should go,
for to you I lift up my soul.

PSALM 143:8

Jesus said, "Not everyone who says to me,
'Lord, Lord,' will enter the kingdom
of heaven, but only he who does the will of
my Father who is in heaven."

MATTHEW 7:21

Put off your old self, which is being
corrupted by its deceitful desires; to be made new
in the attitude of your minds; and to put
on the new self, created to be like God in true
righteousness and holiness.

EPHESIANS 4:22–24

Teach me to do your will,
for you are my God;
may your good Spirit
lead me on level ground.

PSALM 143:10

Father, I pray for a spirit that is willing to be used in your kingdom work. Guide me, Lord. Show me where you want me to serve you. Show me how you want me to do your work. Make me faithful to hear your call and respond with eagerness.

DENISE GEORGE

Never be lacking in zeal, but keep your spiritual fervor, serving the Lord.

ROMANS 12:11

"Acknowledge the God of your father, and serve him with wholehearted devotion and with a willing mind, for the Lord searches every heart and understands every motive behind the thoughts."

1 CHRONICLES 28:9

Always give yourselves fully to the
work of the Lord, because you know that your
labor in the Lord is not in vain.

1 C O R I N T H I A N S 1 5 : 5 8

Jesus said, "Do not work for food
that spoils, but for food that endures to eternal
life, which the Son of Man will
give you. On him God the Father has placed his
seal of approval." Then they asked him,
"What must we do to do the works God requires?"
Jesus answered, "The work of God is this:
to believe in the one he has sent."

J O H N 6 : 2 7 – 2 9

We wait for the blessed hope—
the glorious appearing of our great God and
Savior, Jesus Christ, who gave himself
for us to redeem us from all wickedness and
to purify for himself a people that
are his very own, eager to do what is good.

T I T U S 2 : 1 3 – 1 4

How often do we ignore God's rules for our lives because we're too busy, we're too involved in our own thing, we don't believe, we make up our own rules, or we choose to be downright rebellious? I can imagine God looking at us and saying, "My child, how many times does it take to convince you that my way is the right way? My timing is the perfect timing? My authority is the ultimate authority? My instructions will lead you to a way that has been designed for your good. Why don't you obey me?"

As he questions us, if we're sensitive to listen to his admonishment, we're quick to say, "Father, I'm sorry!" Before the twinkling of an eye, he says, "Forgiven!"

THELMA WELLS

If we confess our sins, he is faithful and just and will forgive us our sins and purify us from all unrighteousness.

1 JOHN 1:9

You are forgiving and good, O Lord,
*   abounding in love to all who call to you.*

PSALM 86:5

You are a forgiving God,
gracious and compassionate, slow to anger
*   and abounding in love.*

NEHEMIAH 9:17

I acknowledged my sin to you
*   and did not cover up my iniquity.*
I said, "I will confess
*   my transgressions to the Lord"—*
and you forgave
*   the guilt of my sin.*

PSALM 32:5

Father God, enable me to bear up under my burden by your grace. Help me to remember that you have handpicked my circumstances to accomplish your purposes for my life. May I humbly submit to your choice for me.

Joni Eareckson Tada

I pray that out of his glorious riches
he may strengthen you with power through
his Spirit in your inner being.

Ephesians 3:16

Humble yourselves before the Lord,
and he will lift you up.

James 4:10

The LORD guides the humble in what is right
and teaches them his way.

PSALM 25:9

The Lord said to me, "My grace is
sufficient for you, for my power is made perfect
in weakness." Therefore I will boast all
the more gladly about my weaknesses, so that
Christ's power may rest on me.
That is why, for Christ's sake, I delight
in weaknesses, in insults, in hardships,
in persecutions, in difficulties.
For when I am weak, then I am strong.

2 CORINTHIANS 12:9−10

We know that in all things God works
for the good of those who love him, who have
been called according to his purpose.

ROMANS 8:28

Give me, O Lord, a steadfast heart, which no
unworthy affection may drag downwards;
give me an unconquered heart, which no
tribulation can wear out; give me an upright
heart, which no unworthy purpose may
tempt aside.

Saint Thomas Aquinas

Create in me a pure heart, O God,
and renew a steadfast spirit within me.
Do not cast me from your presence
or take your Holy Spirit from me.
Restore to me the joy of your salvation
and grant me a willing spirit, to sustain me.

Psalm 51:10–12

"I will give them an undivided heart
and put a new spirit in them; I will remove from
them their heart of stone and give
them a heart of flesh," declares the Lord.

Ezekiel 11:19

My heart is steadfast, O God;
*   I will sing and make music with all my soul.*
For great is your love, higher than the heavens;
*   your faithfulness reaches to the skies.*

PSALM 108:1, 4

*   The God of all grace, who called you*
to his eternal glory in Christ, after you have
suffered a little while, will himself restore you
*   and make you strong, firm and steadfast.*

1 PETER 5:10

O righteous God,
*   who searches minds and hearts,*
bring to an end the violence of the wicked
*   and make the righteous secure.*

PSALM 7:9

As we meditate on God's Word, we become familiar with God's heart and his ways; as we do so, we will change. The purpose of meditation is not simply to make us feel good in a noisy world; it is not a self-absorbed agenda. Rather, as we shut ourselves in with God and reflect on his words, we will know him and be changed by him—and that is the purpose of our lives.

SHEILA WALSH

O God, we meditate on your unfailing love.
Like your name, O God,
   your praise reaches to the ends
     of the earth.
   your right hand is filled with righteousness.

PSALM 48:9–10

I remember the days of long ago;
I meditate on all your works
and consider what your hands have done.
I spread out my hands to you;
my soul thirsts for you like a parched land.

PSALM 143:5–6

I will sing to the LORD all my life;
I will sing praise to my God as long
as I live.
May my meditation be pleasing to him,
as I rejoice in the Lord.

PSALM 104:33–34

Lift my spirits today, Lord, out of my own dilemma, into the light of your presence and provision. Help me look at life in a fresh, exciting way, different from before, being assured that you do not disappoint. I praise you for what you will do in my life today, and I can't wait to see it happen. Amen.

LUCI SWINDOLL

O my God, in you our fathers put their trust;
*   they trusted and you delivered them.*
They cried to you and were saved;
*   in you they trusted and were*
*   not disappointed.*

PSALM 22:4–5

*We do not lose heart. Though outwardly
we are wasting away, yet inwardly we are being
renewed day by day. For our light
and momentary troubles are achieving for us an
eternal glory that far outweighs them all.*

2 CORINTHIANS 4:16–17

*This is the day the LORD has made;
    let us rejoice and be glad in it.
The Lord is God,
    and he has made his light shine upon us.*

PSALM 118:24, 27

*The path of the righteous is like the first gleam
        of dawn,
    shining ever brighter till the full light
        of day.*

PROVERBS 4:18

Good morning, God. I love you! What are you up to today? I want to be a part of it.

NORMAN GRUBB

Let God have your first awaking thoughts; lift up your heart to him reverently and thankfully for the rest enjoyed the night before and cast yourself upon him for the day which follows.

RICHARD BAXTER

Satisfy us in the morning with your
unfailing love,
that we may sing for joy and be glad all
our days.

PSALM 90:14

My dearest Lord,
Be thou a bright flame before me,
Be thou a guiding star above me,
Be thou a smooth path beneath me,
Be thou a kindly shepherd behind me,
Today—tonight—and forever.

SAINT COLUMBA

O LORD, be gracious to us;
*   we long for you.*
Be our strength every morning,
*   our salvation in time of distress.*

ISAIAH 33:2

Father, set me free in the glory of thy will, so that I will only as thou willest. Thy will be at once thy perfection and mine. Thou alone art deliverance—absolute safety from every cause and kind of trouble that ever existed, anywhere now exists, or ever can exist in thy universe.

GEORGE MACDONALD

"Because he loves me," says the LORD, "I will
    rescue him;
  I will protect him, for he acknowledges
    my name.
He will call upon me, and I will answer him;
  I will be with him in trouble,
  I will deliver him and honor him."

PSALM 91:14–15

I will sacrifice a freewill offering to you;
I will praise your name, O LORD,
for it is good.
For he has delivered me from all my troubles,
and my eyes have looked in triumph
on my foes.

PSALM 54:6–7

You are my hiding place;
you will protect me from trouble
and surround me with songs of deliverance.

PSALM 32:7

A righteous man may have many troubles,
but the LORD delivers him from them all.

PSALM 34:19

Dear Lord, thy will be done in everything
and everywhere; without a reserve, without a
but, an if, or a limit.

SAINT FRANCIS OF SALES

From everlasting to everlasting
    the LORD's love is with those who
        fear him,
    and his righteousness with their
        children's children—
with those who keep his covenant
    and remember to obey his precepts.

PSALM 103:17–18

Even when I am old and gray,
    do not forsake me, O God,
till I declare your power to the next generation,
    your might to all who are to come.

PSALM 71:18

We your people, the sheep of your pasture,
will praise you forever;
from generation to generation
we will recount your praise.

PSALM 79:13

How great are his signs,
how mighty his wonders!
His kingdom is an eternal kingdom;
his dominion endures from generation
to generation.

DANIEL 4:3

Though one may be overpowered,
two can defend themselves.
A cord of three strands is not quickly broken.

ECCLESIASTES 4:12

Prayers
FOR *Family*
AND *Friends*

HAPPY THE HOME WHEN GOD IS THERE

Happy the home when God is there,
*   and love fills every breast;*
when one their wish, and one their prayer,
*   and one their heavenly rest.*
Happy the home where Jesus' name
*   is sweet to every ear;*
where children early speak his fame,
*   and parents hold him dear.*

Happy the home where prayer is heard,
and praise is wont to rise;
where parents love the sacred Word
and all its wisdom prize.
Lord, let us in our homes agree
this blessed peace to gain;
unite our hearts in love to thee,
and love to all will reign.

HENRY WARE, JR.

O Lord, bless this household; grant us health and peacefulness, fun and friendship, a warm and welcoming spirit, and the gentleness that quickly forgives, now and always.

AUTHOR UNKNOWN

May the LORD make you increase,
both you and your children.
May you be blessed by the Lord,
the Maker of heaven and earth.

PSALM 115:14–15

Offer hospitality to
one another without grumbling.

1 PETER 4:9

Share with God's people who are in need.
Practice hospitality.

ROMANS 12:13

Train the younger women to love
their husbands and children, to be self-controlled
and pure, to be busy at home, to be kind,
and to be subject to their husbands, so that no
one will malign the word of God.

TITUS 2:4 – 5

The Lord blesses the home of the righteous.

PROVERBS 3:33

My people will live in peaceful dwelling places,
in secure homes,
in undisturbed places of rest.

ISAIAH 32:18

O God, protect those whom we love and who are separated from us. Guide them when they are uncertain, comfort them when they are lonely or afraid, and bless them with the warmth of your presence. Thank you that neither space nor time can cut us off from the love we have in each other and in you.

AUTHOR UNKNOWN

The LORD is near to all who call on him,
    to all who call on him in truth.
He fulfills the desires of those who fear him;
    he hears their cry and saves them.
The LORD watches over all who love him.

PSALM 145:18–20

May the LORD answer you when you are
    in distress;
    may the name of the God of Jacob
    protect you.

PSALM 20:1

I am convinced that neither death nor life,
neither angels nor demons, neither the present
nor the future, nor any powers,
neither height nor depth, nor anything else in
all creation, will be able to separate us from
the love of God that is in Christ Jesus our Lord.

ROMANS 8:38–39

"Because he loves me," says the LORD, *"I will*
rescue him;
I will protect him, for he acknowledges
my name."

PSALM 91:14

Keep me, O LORD, *from the hands of the wicked;*
protect me from men of violence
who plan to trip my feet.

PSALM 140:4

Shielding our loved ones from the consequences of their problems often isn't possible. But praying for their ability to handle those problems is appropriate and can benefit them and us. If you're trying to accept responsibility for the problems of others, pray for them and pray with them—without ceasing.

THELMA WELLS

We constantly pray for you,
that our God may count you worthy of his
calling, and that by his power he may
fulfill every good purpose of yours and every act
prompted by your faith. We pray this so
that the name of our Lord Jesus may be glorified
in you, and you in him, according to the grace
of our God and the Lord Jesus Christ.

2 THESSALONIANS 1:11–12

*I kneel before the Father, from whom his
whole family in heaven and on earth derives its
name. I pray that out of his glorious riches
he may strengthen you with power through his
Spirit in your inner being, so that
Christ may dwell in your hearts through faith.
And I pray that you, being rooted
and established in love, may have power, together
with all the saints, to grasp how wide and
long and high and deep is the love of Christ,
and to know this love that surpasses
knowledge—that you may be filled to the
measure of all the fullness of God.*

EPHESIANS 3:14–19

Pray continually.

1 THESSALONIANS 5:17

BLEST BE THE TIE THAT BINDS

Blest be the tie that binds
    our hearts in Christian love;
the fellowship of kindred minds
    is like to that above.
Before our Father's throne
    we pour our ardent prayers;
our fears, our hopes, our aims are one,
    our comforts and our cares.
We share each other's woes,
    our mutual burdens bear;
and often for each other flows
    the sympathizing tear.
When we asunder part,
    it gives us inward pain;
but we shall still be joined in heart,
    and hope to meet again.

JOHN FAWCETT

May the grace of the Lord Jesus Christ,
and the love of God, and the fellowship of the
Holy Spirit be with you all.

2 Corinthians 13:14

If we walk in the light, as he is in the light,
we have fellowship with one another, and the
blood of Jesus, his Son, purifies us from all sin.

1 John 1:7

Lord God, we offer to you the children living with only one parent. Help them to feel your love, and be with them in their times of confusion and loneliness. Give strength, patience, and wisdom to the parents trying to be both father and mother to the children, at the same time as they face up to their own needs. Help us in the family of the Church to be open and caring with these as with all the families we know, through Jesus Christ our Lord.

CHRISTINE McMULLEN

Sing to God, sing praise to his name,
*   extol him who rides on the clouds—*
his name is the Lord—
*   and rejoice before him.*
A father to the fatherless, a defender of widows,
*   is God in his holy dwelling.*
God sets the lonely in families.

PSALM 68:4–6

Encourage one another and build each other up,
just as in fact you are doing. . . .
Live in peace with each other. And we urge you,
brothers, warn those who are idle,
encourage the timid, help the weak, be patient
with everyone. Pray continually;
give thanks in all circumstances, for this is
God's will for you in Christ Jesus.

1 Thessalonians 5:11, 13–14, 17–18

Arise, Lord! Lift up your hand, O God.
Do not forget the helpless.
But you, O God, do see trouble and grief;
you consider it to take it in hand.
The victim commits himself to you;
you are the helper of the fatherless.

Psalm 10:12, 14

Defend the cause of the weak and fatherless;
maintain the rights of the poor
and oppressed.

Psalm 82:3

Dear Lord, for all in pain
* we pray to thee;*
O come and smite again
* thine enemy.*
Give to thy servants skill
* to soothe and bless,*
And to the tired and ill
* give quietness.*
And, Lord, to those who know
* pain may not cease,*
Come near, that even so
* they may have peace.*

AMY CARMICHAEL

Carry each other's burdens, and in this way
you will fulfill the law of Christ.

GALATIANS 6:2

*Praise be to the God and Father of our
Lord Jesus Christ, the Father of compassion and
the God of all comfort, who comforts us
in all our troubles, so that we can comfort those
in any trouble with the comfort we ourselves
have received from God.*

2 CORINTHIANS 1:3–4

*"Peace, peace, to those far and near,"
says the LORD. "And I will heal them."*

ISAIAH 57:19

*I will listen to what God the LORD will say;
he promises peace to his people, his saints.*

PSALM 85:8

Dear Lord, I do not ask that thou should'st give me
some high work of thine, some noble calling
or some wondrous task;
Give me a little hand to hold in mine;
Give me a little child to point the way
over the strange, sweet path that leads to thee.
Give me two shining eyes thy face to see.
The only crown I ask, dear Lord, to wear is this:
that I may teach my little child.
I do not ask that I may ever stand
among the wise, the worthy, or the great;
I only ask that softly, hand in hand,
my child and I may enter at the gate.

AUTHOR UNKNOWN

Fix these words of mine in your hearts
and minds; tie them as symbols on your hands
and bind them on your foreheads.
Teach them to your children, talking about them
when you sit at home and when you walk
along the road, when you lie down and when
you get up. Write them on the doorframes of
your houses and on your gates, so that your days
and the days of your children may
be many in the land that the Lord swore to give
your forefathers, as many as the days that the
heavens are above the earth.

DEUTERONOMY 11:18–21

May your father and mother be glad;
may she who gave you birth rejoice!

PROVERBS 23:25

Daddy God: Thank you for applauding our being childlike, for it's such fun and so restorative—not just as we play ballerina on our tiptoes, but as we, in childlike spontaneity, reach up to you. May we learn to be deliberately generous in extending opportunities to others to know your parental care. As we stuff our bags full of goodies (peace, patience, love, joy), may we then share them lavishly. Thank you for always sticking by us. Amen.

PATSY CLAIRMONT

I write to you, dear children,
because your sins have been forgiven on account
of his name. ...I write to you, dear children,
because you have known the Father.

1 JOHN 2:12−13

From birth I have relied on you;
you brought me forth from my mother's womb.
I will ever praise you.

PSALM 71:6

From birth I was cast upon you;
*   from my mother's womb you have been*
*   my God.*

PSALM 22:10

Jesus said, "I praise you, Father,
Lord of heaven and earth, because you have
hidden these things from the wise and learned,
and revealed them to little children. Yes, Father,
*   for this was your good pleasure."*

MATTHEW 11:25–26

Jesus called a little child and had him
*   stand among them. And he said:*
"I tell you the truth, unless you change and
*   become like little children,*
you will never enter the kingdom of heaven.
*   Therefore, whoever humbles himself*
like this child is the greatest in the kingdom
*   of heaven. And whoever welcomes*
*   a little child like this*
*   in my name welcomes me."*

MATTHEW 18:2–5

JESUS, UNITED BY THY GRACE

Jesus, united by thy grace
        and each to each endeared,
with confidence we seek thy face
        and know our prayer is heard.
Help us to help each other, Lord,
        each other's cross to bear;
let all their friendly aid afford,
        and feel each other's care.
Up unto thee, our living Head,
        let us in all things grow;
till thou hast made us free
        indeed and spotless here below.

Touched by the lodestone of thy love,
  let all our hearts agree,
and ever toward each other move,
  and ever move toward thee.
To thee, inseparably joined,
  let all our spirits cleave;
O may we all the loving mind
  that was in thee receive.
This is the bond of perfectness,
  thy spotless charity;
O let us, still we pray, possess
  the mind that was in thee.

CHARLES WESLEY

Master, you did some unusual things during your walk here on earth. People thought you were a bit strange. Teach us to love everybody regardless of their ethnic origin, religion, geographic location, educational status, financial ability, social standing, personality, or physical ability. And when we want to ignore or move away from people we don't understand, help us to listen to our instincts and not to miss out on some of the best blessings—even when they come in unusual packages.

THELMA WELLS

You are all sons of God through faith
in Christ Jesus. There is neither Jew nor Greek,
slave nor free, male nor female,
for you are all one in Christ Jesus.

GALATIANS 3:26, 28

*As believers in our glorious Lord Jesus Christ,
don't show favoritism. Suppose a man comes into
your meeting wearing a gold ring and
fine clothes, and a poor man in shabby clothes
also comes in. If you show special
attention to the man wearing fine clothes and
say, "Here's a good seat for you," but say
to the poor man, "You stand there" or
"Sit on the floor by my feet," have you not
discriminated among yourselves?*

JAMES 2:1–4

*We were all baptized by one Spirit into
one body—whether Jews or Greeks, slave or free—
and we were all given the one Spirit to drink.*

1 CORINTHIANS 12:13

O God, the Spirit of truth, help us to be truthful with one another. O God, the Spirit of gentleness, help us to be gentle with one another. O God, who knows what is in our hearts more clearly than we do ourselves, help us to hear one another. O God, lead us in the way of truth and love.

RICHARD HARRIES

*Confess your sins to each other and
pray for each other so that you may be healed.
The prayer of a righteous
man is powerful and effective.*

JAMES 5:16

*Be completely humble and gentle; be patient,
bearing with one another in love.*

EPHESIANS 4:2

As God's chosen people, holy and dearly loved,
clothe yourselves with compassion,
kindness, humility, gentleness and patience.

COLOSSIANS 3:12

Speaking the truth in love, we will in all things
grow up into him who is the Head,
that is, Christ. From him the whole body,
joined and held together by every
supporting ligament, grows and builds itself
up in love, as each part does its work.

EPHESIANS 4:15–16

Pursue righteousness, godliness,
faith, love, endurance and gentleness.

1 TIMOTHY 6:11

Dear Lord Jesus, we commit ourselves and our loved ones into your hands. We want to be good forgivers—expert forgivers like you are. What we cannot manage to forgive this moment, help us to move toward one degree at a time. Amen.

BARBARA JOHNSON

Jesus said, "So watch yourselves.
If your brother sins, rebuke him, and if he repents,
forgive him. If he sins against you
seven times in a day, and seven times comes back
to you and says, 'I repent,' forgive him."

LUKE 17:3–4

Now instead, you ought to forgive and
comfort him, so that he will not be overwhelmed
by excessive sorrow. I urge you,
therefore, to reaffirm your love for him.

2 CORINTHIANS 2:7–8

The Lord is not slow in keeping his promise,
as some understand slowness.
He is patient with you, not wanting anyone to
perish, but everyone to come to repentance.

2 PETER 3:9

Accept one another, then, just as Christ
accepted you, in order to bring praise to God.

ROMANS 15:7

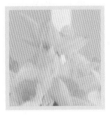

Jesus taught his disciples to pray,
"Forgive us our debts,
as we also have forgiven our debtors."

MATTHEW 6:12

Jesus said, "Blessed are the merciful,
for they will be shown mercy."

MATTHEW 5:7

Are you dealing with someone whom you feel will never change? Do you vacillate between wishing he would change and just wanting him to leave you alone? Have you given up expecting good things from that person? Nobody is so far from God that he can't get back to the Lord. Our responsibility is to keep knocking at God's door about that person, to keep believing God will answer our prayers. Thank God for what He will do. Patiently but expectantly wait on the Lord. Renew your hope!

THELMA WELLS

He is able to save completely those who come to God through him, because he always lives to intercede for them.

HEBREWS 7:25

*I urge, then, first of all, that requests,
prayers, intercession and thanksgiving be made
for everyone. This is good, and pleases God
our Savior, who wants all men to be saved and
to come to a knowledge of the truth.*

1 TIMOTHY 2:1, 3–4

*Abraham did not waver through unbelief
regarding the promise of God,
but was strengthened in his faith and gave
glory to God, being fully persuaded that God
had power to do what he had promised.*

ROMANS 4:20–21

*Hope does not disappoint us, because God
has poured out his love into our hearts by the
Holy Spirit, whom he has given us.
You see, at just the right time, when we were still
powerless, Christ died for the ungodly. But God
demonstrates his own love for us in this:
While we were still sinners, Christ died for us.*

ROMANS 5:5–6, 8

Give us, we pray you, gentle God, a mind
forgetful of past injury, a will to seek the
good of others, and a heart of love.

A NEW ZEALAND PRAYER BOOK

*The mind of sinful man is death, but the
mind controlled by the Spirit is life and peace.*

ROMANS 8:6

*Do not conform any longer to the
pattern of this world, but be transformed by the
renewing of your mind.*

ROMANS 12:2

It was God who gave some to be apostles,
some to be prophets, some to
be evangelists, and some to be pastors and
teachers, to prepare God's people
for works of service, so that the body of Christ
may be built up until we all reach unity
in the faith and in the knowledge of the Son of
God and become mature, attaining to
the whole measure of the fullness of Christ.

EPHESIANS 4:11–13

Finally, brothers, whatever is true,
whatever is noble, whatever is right, whatever is
pure, whatever is lovely, whatever is admirable—
if anything is excellent or praiseworthy—
think about such things.

PHILIPPIANS 4:8

Lord, what we know not, teach us.
Lord, what we have not, give us.
Lord, what we are not, make us.

SAINT AUGUSTINE OF HIPPO

Do not forget my teaching,
but keep my commands in your heart,
for they will prolong your life many years
and bring you prosperity.

PROVERBS 3:1–2

Since my youth, O God, you have taught me,
and to this day I declare your
marvelous deeds.

PSALM 71:17

O God our Savior,
You care for the land and water it;
   you enrich it abundantly.
The streams of God are filled with water
   to provide the people with grain,
   for so you have ordained it.
You drench its furrows
   and level its ridges;
you soften it with showers
   and bless its crops.
You crown the year with your bounty,
   and your carts overflow with abundance.

PSALM 65:9–11

My God will meet all your needs
according to his glorious riches in Christ Jesus.

PHILIPPIANS 4:19

Lord, help us to listen to each other, to be gentle with one another, to forgive each other, and to be willing to laugh at ourselves.

AUTHOR UNKNOWN

Be kind and compassionate
to one another, forgiving each other, just as
in Christ God forgave you.

EPHESIANS 4:32

Jesus said, "Do not judge, and you
will not be judged. Do not condemn, and you
will not be condemned. Forgive,
and you will be forgiven. Give, and it will
be given to you. A good measure, pressed down,
shaken together and running over, will be poured
into your lap. For with the measure you use,
it will be measured to you."

LUKE 6:37–38

The wisdom that comes from heaven is
first of all pure; then peace-loving, considerate,
submissive, full of mercy and good fruit,
impartial and sincere. Peacemakers who sow in
peace raise a harvest of righteousness.

JAMES 3:17–18

Remind the people to be subject to rulers
and authorities, to be obedient, to be ready to do
whatever is good, to slander no one,
to be peaceable and considerate, and to show
true humility toward all men.

TITUS 3:1–2

"God will yet fill your mouth with laughter
and your lips with shouts of joy."

JOB 8:21

Father, what an incredible display of your
sovereignty—your plans are not thwarted.
I rejoice that no angel, person, or circumstance
can stop your plan for my life or for my
children. Nothing occurs in our lives without
your divine permission, and for that I am
thankful. Thank you for allowing the
difficulties in our lives to make us more
like Jesus.

FERN NICHOLS

"These are the words of him who is
holy and true, who holds the key of David.
What he opens no one can shut, and what he
shuts no one can open. I know your deeds.
See, I have placed before you an open door that
no one can shut. I know that you have
little strength, yet you have kept my word and
have not denied my name."

REVELATION 3:7–8

I was young and now I am old,
yet I have never seen the righteous forsaken
or their children begging bread.
They are always generous and lend freely;
their children will be blessed.

PSALM 37:25–26

*"O Sovereign LORD, you have begun
to show to your servant your greatness and your
strong hand. For what god is there in heaven
or on earth who can do the deeds
and mighty works you do?"*

DEUTERONOMY 3:24

*I am not saying this because I am in need,
for I have learned to be content whatever the
circumstances. I know what it is to be
in need, and I know what it is to have plenty.
I have learned the secret of being content in any
and every situation, whether well fed
or hungry, whether living in plenty or in want.*

PHILIPPIANS 4:11–12

When we pray for one another, we begin to love one another. In the biblical sense, intercession is prayer made on behalf of another person for his best interests. This is an act of love in which the intercessor names that person, sometimes with a specific request, at other times just surrounding that person with God's unconditional love.

ROSALIND RINKER

Pray in the Spirit on all occasions with all kinds of prayers and requests. With this in mind, be alert and always keep on praying for all the saints.

EPHESIANS 6:18

May the Lord make your love increase and overflow for each other and for everyone else, just as ours does for you.

1 THESSALONIANS 3:12

*Jesus said, "My command is this: Love each
other as I have loved you. Greater love
has no one than this, that he lay down
his life for his friends."*

JOHN 15:12–13

*The prayer offered in faith will make
the sick person well; the Lord will raise him up.
If he has sinned, he will be forgiven.*

JAMES 5:15

*Help us by your prayers. Then many will give
thanks on our behalf for the gracious favor
granted us in answer to the prayers of many.*

2 CORINTHIANS 1:11

*Devote yourselves to prayer,
being watchful and thankful.*

COLOSSIANS 4:2

Lord, teach me to forget myself and love
others. Amen.

S H E I L A   W A L S H

*Serve wholeheartedly,
as if you were serving the Lord, not men.*

E P H E S I A N S   6 : 7

*Jesus said, "The greatest among you
will be your servant. For whoever exalts himself
will be humbled, and whoever
humbles himself will be exalted."*

M A T T H E W   2 3 : 1 1 – 1 2

*You ... were called to be free.
But do not use your freedom to indulge the sinful
nature; rather, serve one another in love.*

G A L A T I A N S   5 : 1 3

*Love each other deeply, because love
covers over a multitude of sins. Offer hospitality
to one another without grumbling. Each one
should use whatever gift he has received to serve
others, faithfully administering God's grace in
its various forms. If anyone speaks, he should do
it as one speaking the very words of God.*

1 PETER 4:8–11

*In Christ we who are many form one body,
and each member belongs to all
the others. We have different gifts, according
to the grace given us.... If a man's gift
is prophesying, let him use it in proportion to
his faith. If it is serving, let him serve;
if it is teaching, let him teach; if it is encouraging,
let him encourage; if it is contributing to the
needs of others, let him give generously;
if it is leadership, let him govern diligently; if it
is showing mercy, let him do it cheerfully.*

ROMANS 12:5–8

You, Lord, are our champion. Teach us to
value people even more than the tantalizing
last word. May we lean in and truly hear
each other. Amen.

PATSY CLAIRMONT

*Jesus said, "I tell you: Love your enemies
and pray for those who persecute you, that you
may be sons of your Father in heaven.
He causes his sun to rise on the evil and the
good, and sends rain on the righteous
and the unrighteous. If you love those who love
you, what reward will you get?"*

MATTHEW 5:44–46

He who holds his tongue is wise.

PROVERBS 10:19

*A man who lacks judgment derides his neighbor,
but a man of understanding holds
his tongue.*

PROVERBS 11:12

*Bless those who persecute you; bless and
do not curse. Do not repay anyone evil for evil.
Be careful to do what is right in the eyes
of everybody. If it is possible, as far as it depends
on you, live at peace with everyone. Do not
take revenge.... On the contrary: If your enemy
is hungry, feed him; if he is thirsty,
give him something to drink.... Do not be
overcome by evil, but overcome evil with good.*

ROMANS 12:14, 17–21

*Do not let any unwholesome talk come out
of your mouths, but only what is helpful for
building others up according to their needs, that
it may benefit those who listen.*

EPHESIANS 4:29

The tongue that brings healing is a tree of life.

PROVERBS 15:4

O Lord, how awesome you are. Just one touch of your garment can make the most defiled clean. You know all about what we encounter every day. You know the negatives that surround us at home, at work, at school, at church, in the community, and in our minds. Please remind us that if we continue to press toward you without giving up, you will surely heal and deliver us from our anguish. Help us to encourage others to lean on you when they seem discouraged by this world's troubles. Let us be an example by seeking comfort and peace in Jesus' presence. For in his presence is joy beyond measure. Amen.

THELMA WELLS

Jesus said, "Go home to your family and tell them how much the Lord has done for you, and how he has had mercy on you."

MARK 5:19

*In everything set them an example
by doing what is good. In your teaching show
integrity, seriousness.*

TITUS 2:7

*Don't let anyone look down
on you because you are young, but set an
example for the believers in speech, in life,
in love, in faith and in purity.*

1 TIMOTHY 4:12

*"Come now, let us reason together,"
says the LORD.
"Though your sins are like scarlet,
they shall be as white as snow;
though they are red as crimson,
they shall be like wool."*

ISAIAH 1:18

Dear Lord, never let me be afraid to pray for the impossible.

DOROTHY SHELLENBERGER

Jesus said, "In that day you will no longer ask me anything. I tell you the truth, my Father will give you whatever you ask in my name. Until now you have not asked for anything in my name. Ask and you will receive, and your joy will be complete."

JOHN 16:23–24

Jesus looked at them and said,
"With man this is impossible, but not with God;
all things are possible with God."

MARK 10:27

Let us then approach the throne of grace
with confidence, so that we may receive mercy and
find grace to help us in our time of need.

HEBREWS 4:16

On God we have set our hope that
he will continue to deliver us, as you help us by
your prayers. Then many will give thanks on
our behalf for the gracious favor granted us in
answer to the prayers of many.

2 CORINTHIANS 1:10–11

Give thanks to the LORD, call on his name;
    make known among the nations what
    he has done.
Sing to him, sing praise to him;
    tell of all his wonderful acts.
Glory in his holy name;
    let the hearts of those who seek the
    LORD rejoice.
Look to the Lord and his strength;
    seek his face always.
Remember the wonders he has done,
    his miracles.

1 CHRONICLES 16:8–12

Time is in your hands, Lord. Help me to
remember that when the line in the grocery
store is long, the phone won't stop ringing,
or a friend indicates she needs to talk.
Remind me to relax so I can be part of
anything amazing you might want to do
through me or for me.

JONI EARECKSON TADA

An anxious heart weighs a man down,
*   but a kind word cheers him up.*

PROVERBS 12:25

Jesus said, "Peace I leave with you;
my peace I give you. I do not give to you as the
world gives. Do not let your
hearts be troubled and do not be afraid."

JOHN 14:27

There is a time for everything,
and a season for every activity under heaven.

ECCLESIASTES 3:1

Why are you downcast, O my soul?
    Why so disturbed within me?
Put your hope in God,
    for I will yet praise him,
        my Savior and my God.

PSALM 42:5–6

Prayers
OF *Joy* AND
Celebration

To be blessed is to be happy. Actually, scholars use the word *blissful* for *blessed*. Exultant and joyous, radiant and rapturous. God is not a threatened, pacing deity starving for attention. He is not easily angered, touchy, or out of sorts on bad days. He is not biting his nails or blowing his stack when the world goes awry. Rather he is the exultant and rapturously happy God.

Jesus had in mind joy and happiness when he said, "Blessed are the poor ... the meek ... the peacemakers" (Mathew 5:3, 5, 9). He meant that such people are divinely favored; they are smiled upon; they are truly the delightfully contented ones. We are most like God when we are full of joy—godly joy that overflows from meekness, humility, and spiritual poverty—that is, a deep awareness of our desperate need of him.

JONI EARECKSON TADA

The Lord is compassionate and gracious,
slow to anger, abounding in love.

In the east give glory to the Lord;
exalt the name of the Lord, the God
of Israel,
in the islands of the sea.
From the ends of the earth we hear singing:
"Glory to the Righteous One."

May the righteous be glad
and rejoice before God;
may they be happy and joyful.

Lord Jesus, without our knowledge of you and salvation from you, we would be unable to truly "hear joy" or feel gladness. You are the source of our peace, the foundation upon which our security rests, and the inspiration for finding gladness in the dailyness of our lives. May we experience more God-given gladness as we celebrate the days you have ordained for us here on earth. Amen.

MARILYN MEBERG

Shout for joy to the LORD, all the earth.
       Worship the LORD with gladness;
       come before him with joyful songs.
Know that the LORD is God.
       It is he who made us, and we are his;
       we are his people, the sheep of his pasture.

PSALM 100:1–3

I will exalt you, O L<small>ORD</small>,
    for you lifted me out of the depths
        and did not let my enemies gloat over me.
O Lord my God, I called to you for help
    and you healed me.
O Lord, you brought me up from the grave;
        you spared me from going down into the pit.
Sing to the L<small>ORD</small>, you saints of his;
    praise his holy name.

P S A L M   3 0 : 1 – 4

Moses and the Israelites sang this song to the L<small>ORD</small>:
"I will sing to the L<small>ORD</small>,
    for he is highly exalted.
The horse and its rider
    he has hurled into the sea.
The Lord is my strength and my song;
    he has become my salvation.
He is my God, and I will praise him,
        my father's God, and I will exalt him."

E X O D U S   1 5 : 1 – 2

Father, give me the grace today to take time.
Time to be with you. Time to be with
others. Time to enjoy the life you have given
me. Help me remember that today is the day
you have made. May I rejoice and be glad in
it! Amen.

Luci Swindoll

As the deer pants for streams of water,
    so my soul pants for you, O God.
My soul thirsts for God, for the living God.
    When can I go and meet with God?

Psalm 42:1–2

You have made known to me the path of life;
    you will fill me with joy in your presence,
    with eternal pleasures at your right hand.

Psalm 16:11

I sought the LORD, and he answered me;
  he delivered me from all my fears.
Those who look to him are radiant;
  their faces are never covered with shame.

PSALM 34:4–5

Jesus said, "When you pray, go into your room,
  close the door and pray to your Father,
who is unseen. Then your Father, who sees what
  is done in secret, will reward you."

MATTHEW 6:6

Reach out for God and find him,
though he is not far from each one of us.

ACTS 17:27

O Lord, because of your life in me, each moment of my life has value and potential for significance—if I will only celebrate it. Infuse my attitude with the fruit of your Spirit, patience. Amen.

BARBARA JOHNSON

The fruit of the Spirit is love, joy, peace, patience, kindness, goodness, faithfulness, gentleness and self-control.
Against such things there is no law.

GALATIANS 5:22−23

Surely goodness and love will follow me all the days of my life, and I will dwell in the house of the Lord forever.

PSALM 23:6

*Your attitude should be the same
as that of Christ Jesus:
Who, being in very nature God,
did not consider equality
with God something to be grasped,
but made himself nothing,
taking the very nature of a servant.*

PHILIPPIANS 2:5–7

*Yet, O LORD, you are our Father.
We are the clay, you are the potter;
we are all the work of your hand.*

ISAIAH 64:8

*Jesus said, "I have come that
they may have life, and have it to the full."*

JOHN 10:10

Thank you, Lord, that we are glory bound.
Hallelujah!

PATSY CLAIRMONT

*Jesus said, "Rejoice that
your names are written in heaven."*

LUKE 10:20

*In keeping with his promise we are
looking forward to a new heaven and a new
earth, the home of righteousness.*

2 PETER 3:13

*Jesus said, "Blessed are those who wash their
robes, that they may have the right to the tree of
life and may go through the gates into the city."*

REVELATION 22:14

Many, O LORD my God,
  are the wonders you have done.
The things you planned for us
  no one can recount to you;
were I to speak and tell of them,
  they would be too many to declare.

PSALM 40:5

The criminal on the cross said, "Jesus, remember
  me when you come into your kingdom."
Jesus answered him, "I tell you the truth, today
  you will be with me in paradise."

LUKE 23:42–43

Eternal Father, through your Spirit delighting in the world, you created us from joy and for joy: grant us a deeper knowledge of the joy which is ours in Christ Jesus, that here our hearts may be glad, and in the world to come our joy may be full: for with the Son and the Holy Spirit, you are our God, now and for ever.

RAYMOND HOCKLEY

Though you have not seen him,
you love him; and even though you do not see
him now, you believe in him and
are filled with an inexpressible and glorious joy,
for you are receiving the goal
of your faith, the salvation of your souls.

1 PETER 1:8–9

My lips will shout for joy
when I sing praise to you—
I, whom you have redeemed.

PSALM 71:23

The Lord your God will bless you
in all your harvest and in all the work of your
hands, and your joy will be complete.

DEUTERONOMY 16:15

Splendor and majesty are before him;
strength and joy in his dwelling place.

1 CHRONICLES 16:27

To the only God our Savior be glory,
majesty, power and authority, through Jesus
Christ our Lord, before all ages,
now and forevermore! Amen.

JUDE 1:25

Sing joyfully to the LORD, you righteous;
it is fitting for the upright to praise him.

PSALM 33:1

Lord, teach us to "banish anxiety from our hearts and cast off the troubles of our bodies." Thank you for the assurance of your love for us, which releases us to live out joyful impulses. Create within us a lightness of being that comes from knowing you. Amen.

MARILYN MEBERG

Banish anxiety from your heart
and cast off the troubles of your body.

ECCLESIASTES 11:10

When anxiety was great within me,
your consolation brought joy to my soul.

PSALM 94:19

The LORD is a refuge for the oppressed,
a stronghold in times of trouble

PSALM 9:9

In the day of trouble
he will keep me safe in his dwelling;
he will hide me in the shelter of his tabernacle
and set me high upon a rock.

PSALM 27:5

Since we have such a hope, we are
very bold. We are not like Moses, who would put
a veil over his face to keep the Israelites
from gazing at it while the radiance was fading
away. But whenever anyone turns
to the Lord, the veil is taken away. Now the Lord
is the Spirit, and where the Spirit of the
Lord is, there is freedom. And we, who with
unveiled faces all reflect the Lord's glory,
are being transformed into his
likeness with ever-increasing glory,
which comes from the Lord, who is the Spirit.

2 CORINTHIANS 3:12–13, 16–18

Blessing and honour, thanksgiving and praise,
more than I can utter, more than I can
understand, be yours, O most glorious Trinity,
Father, Son, and Holy Spirit, by all angels, all
people, all creatures, now and for ever.

LANCELOT ANDREWES

I will extol the LORD at all times;
   his praise will always be on my lips.
My soul will boast in the LORD;
   let the afflicted hear and rejoice.
Glorify the LORD with me;
   let us exalt his name together.

PSALM 34:1–3

Enter his gates with thanksgiving
   and his courts with praise;
   give thanks to him and praise his name.

PSALM 100:4

I will praise you, O LORD, among the nations;
I will sing of you among the peoples.
For great is your love, higher than the heavens;
your faithfulness reaches to the skies.
Be exalted, O God, above the heavens,
and let your glory be over all the earth.

PSALM 108:3-5

I looked and heard the voice of many angels,
numbering thousands upon thousands,
and ten thousand times ten thousand. They
encircled the throne and the living
creatures and the elders. In a loud voice they sang:
"Worthy is the Lamb, who was slain,
to receive power and wealth and wisdom
and strength
and honor and glory and praise!"

REVELATION 5:11-12

Dear Lord Jesus, there's so much in life that isn't fun, that hurts and drags us down. Give us the eyes to focus on the stray joys that could so easily slip past us. Help us widen our vision to not only encompass those "joy breaks," but to see the ways in which we can bring them to others in whatever stage of life they may be. Amen.

MARILYN MEBERG

Those who sow in tears
will reap with songs of joy.
He who goes out weeping,
carrying seed to sow,
will return with songs of joy,
carrying sheaves with him.

PSALM 126:5–6

I am still confident of this:
I will see the goodness of the Lord
in the land of the living.

PSALM 27:13

I lift up my eyes to the hills—
*   where does my help come from?*
My help comes from the Lord,
*   the Maker of heaven and earth.*
He will not let your foot slip—
*   he who watches over you will not slumber.*

                PSALM 121:1–3

May God give you the desire of your heart
*   and make all your plans succeed.*
We will shout for joy when you are victorious
*   and will lift up our banners in the name*
*   of our God.*
May the LORD grant all your requests.

                PSALM 20:4–5

Dear Lord Jesus, make me aware of your
precious treasure that is all around me. Your
Word says you have given me more than
enough. I celebrate my heritage as your
child. Amen.

BARBARA JOHNSON

The house of the righteous contains great treasure.

PROVERBS 15:6

We are children of God, and what we will be
has not yet been made known. But we
know that when he appears, we shall be like
him, for we shall see him as he is.

1 JOHN 3:2

If you accept my words
     and store up my commands within you,
turning your ear to wisdom
     and applying your heart to understanding,
and if you call out for insight
     and cry aloud for understanding,
and if you look for it as for silver
     and search for it as for hidden treasure,
then you will understand the fear of the LORD
     and find the knowledge of God.
For the LORD gives wisdom,
     and from his mouth come
          knowledge and understanding.

PROVERBS 2:1–6

We have joy, dear Father, because we can take refuge in you. You provide our safety, our security, our eternal hope. Because of those loving assurances, enable us to see the joy, feel the joy, and even twirl with joy. Thank you that you are our reason for joy each day. Amen.

MARILYN MEBERG

"May those who love you be secure.
May there be peace within your walls
    and security within your citadels."
For the sake of my brothers and friends,
    I will say, "Peace be within you."
For the sake of the house of the LORD our God,
    I will seek your prosperity.

PSALM 122:6–9

The LORD is my rock, my fortress and my deliverer;
my God is my rock, in whom I take refuge.
He is my shield and the horn of my
salvation, my stronghold.

PSALM 18:2

You have filled my heart with greater joy
than when their grain and new
wine abound.
I will lie down and sleep in peace,
for you alone, O LORD,
make me dwell in safety.

PSALM 4:7 – 8

Whoever listens to me will live in safety
and be at ease, without fear of harm.

PROVERBS 1:33

Lord, I'm so grateful you designed us with the capability to giggle. What a pleasing sound. And what a delightful feeling. Help us to be generous with our giggles and sparse with our frowns. In the pleasing name of Jesus, amen.

PATSY CLAIRMONT

He brought out his people with rejoicing,
his chosen ones with shouts of joy.

PSALM 105:43

Then my soul will rejoice in the LORD
and delight in his salvation.

PSALM 35:9

The cheerful heart has a continual feast.

PROVERBS 15:15

I was filled with delight day after day,
    rejoicing always in his presence,
rejoicing in his whole world
    and delighting in mankind.

PROVERBS 8:30–31

I delight greatly in the LORD;
    my soul rejoices in my God.
For he has clothed me with garments of salvation
    and arrayed me in a robe of righteousness,
as a bridegroom adorns his head like a priest,
    and as a bride adorns herself with
        her jewels.

ISAIAH 61:10

Creator of joy, help me this very day to look around and find something to laugh about. Doesn't have to be big. Doesn't have to be unusual. Just some little thing to remind me you are a God of jubilation. Keep me from being a stick in the mud! Help me to have fun today, and not put it off until tomorrow. Amen.

LUCI SWINDOLL

Our mouths were filled with laughter,
our tongues with songs of joy.
Then it was said among the nations,
"The LORD has done great things for them."

PSALM 126:2

A cheerful heart is good medicine.

PROVERBS 17:22

He put a new song in my mouth,
a hymn of praise to our God.

PSALM 40:3

A cheerful look brings joy to the heart,
and good news gives health to the bones.

PROVERBS 15:30

Shout for joy to the LORD, all the earth,
burst into jubilant song with music;
make music to the LORD with the harp,
with the harp and the sound of singing.

PSALM 98:4–5

Let the heavens rejoice, let the earth be glad;
let them say among the nations,
"The Lord reigns!"
Let the sea resound, and all that is in it;
let the fields be jubilant, and everything
in them!

2 CHRONICLES 16:31–32

O God in heaven, you love us so completely that you even provide a means by which we can be released from pain and discouragement through laughter. How mind-bogglingly creative! Help us to rise up out of the dark corners of our soul and believe you have indeed provided medicine for joyful healing. May we take at least one dose every day. Amen.

MARILYN MEBERG

Then your light will break forth like the dawn,
and your healing will quickly appear;
then your righteousness will go before you,
and the glory of the Lord will be your
rear guard.

ISAIAH 58:8

The LORD says, "I will heal my people and will let them enjoy abundant peace and security."

JEREMIAH 33:6

*For you who revere my name, the sun
of righteousness will rise with healing in its
wings. And you will go out and
leap like calves released from the stall.*

MALACHI 4:2

*News about Jesus spread all over Syria,
and people brought to him all who were ill with
various diseases, those suffering severe pain,
the demon-possessed, those having seizures, and
the paralyzed, and he healed them.*

MATTHEW 4:24

*God reached down from on high and took hold
of me;
he drew me out of deep waters.*

PSALM 18:16

*You, O LORD, keep my lamp burning;
my God turns my darkness into light.*

PSALM 18:28

O Lord, as I think about joy and fun, I am
reminded of 1 Timothy 6:17 that instructs
us not to trust in the uncertainty of wealth
but to put our hope in God, who richly
provides us with everything for our
enjoyment. Thank you for the laughter you
create in the fellowship of being together
with those we love. It is a gift of your grace.
Amen.

LUCI SWINDOLL

*Command those who are rich in this
present world not to be arrogant nor to put their
hope in wealth, which is so uncertain,
but to put their hope in God, who richly provides us with everything for our enjoyment.*

1 TIMOTHY 6:17

*They devoted themselves to the apostles'
teaching and to the fellowship, to the breaking
of bread and to prayer.*

ACTS 2:42

*Since we have been justified through faith,
we have peace with God through our Lord Jesus
Christ, through whom we have gained access
by faith into this grace in which we now stand.
And we rejoice in the hope of the glory of God.*

ROMANS 5:1-2

*If you have any encouragement from
being united with Christ, if any comfort from his
love, if any fellowship with the Spirit, if any
tenderness and compassion, then make my joy
complete by being like-minded, having the same
love, being one in spirit and purpose.*

PHILIPPIANS 2:1-2

Dear Lord, you gave us a funny bone so we would use it. You gave us belly and facial muscles with which to laugh. I won't let them atrophy. I'll laugh with you and for you today. Amen.

BARBARA JOHNSON

A happy heart makes the face cheerful.

PROVERBS 15:13

Let all who take refuge in you be glad;
    let them ever sing for joy.
Spread your protection over them,
        that those who love your name may rejoice
        in you.

PSALM 5:11

Maidens will dance and be glad,
young men and old as well.
I will turn their mourning into gladness;
I will give them comfort and joy instead
of sorrow.

JEREMIAH 31:13

Praise him with the sounding of the trumpet,
praise him with the harp and lyre,
praise him with tambourine and dancing,
praise him with the strings and flute,
praise him with the clash of cymbals,
praise him with resounding cymbals.
Let everything that has breath praise the LORD.
Praise the LORD.

PSALM 150:3−6

Jesus, help me to see the humor in everyday occurrences. And when I make mistakes, remind me it isn't the end of the world. It's a learning experience, an opportunity to laugh and to trust your sovereignty. Amen.

LUCI SWINDOLL

If the LORD delights in a man's way,
*   he makes his steps firm;*
though he stumble, he will not fall,
*   for the LORD upholds him with his hand.*

PSALM 37:23–24

We all stumble in many ways.

JAMES 3:2

When the disciples saw him walking
on the lake, they were terrified. "It's a ghost,"
they said, and cried out in fear.
But Jesus immediately said to them: "Take
courage! It is I. Don't be afraid." "Lord, if it's you,"
Peter replied, "tell me to come to you
on the water." "Come," he said. Then Peter got
down out of the boat, walked on the water
and came toward Jesus. But when he saw the wind,
he was afraid and, beginning to sink,
cried out, "Lord, save me!" Immediately Jesus
reached out his hand and caught him.

MATTHEW 14:26–31

Not that I have already obtained all this,
or have already been made perfect,
but I press on to take hold of that for which
Christ Jesus took hold of me.

PHILIPPIANS 3:12

Lord Jesus, without you, our laughter would quickly become hollow and meaningless. But you give us reason for being, you give us significance in being, and you fill our being with the awesome assurance that we have been cleansed and forgiven of all sin. Because of the cross, we have been reconciled to you for now and eternity. Because of that truth, we do indeed break forth with rejoicing and shouts of joy. Amen.

MARILYN MEBERG

Once you were alienated from God and were enemies in your minds because of your evil behavior. But now he has reconciled you by Christ's physical body through death to present you holy in his sight, without blemish and free from accusation—if you continue in your faith, established and firm.

COLOSSIANS 1:21–23

If anyone is in Christ, he is a new creation;
the old has gone, the new has come!
All this is from God, who reconciled us to
himself through Christ and gave us the ministry
of reconciliation: that God was reconciling
the world to himself in Christ, not counting
men's sins against them. And he has
committed to us the message of reconciliation.
We are therefore Christ's ambassadors, as though
God were making his appeal through us.
We implore you on Christ's behalf: Be reconciled
to God. God made him who had no sin
to be sin for us, so that in him we might
become the righteousness of God.

2 CORINTHIANS 5:17–21

If, when we were God's enemies,
we were reconciled to him through the death of
his Son, how much more, having been
reconciled, shall we be saved through his life!

ROMANS 5:10

O God, for your love for us, warm and brooding,
*   which has brought us to birth and opened*
*   our eyes*
to the wonder and beauty of creation,
*   we give you thanks.*

For your love for us, compassionate and patient,
*   which has carried us through our pain,*
wept beside us in our sin,
*   and waited with us in our confusion,*
we give you thanks.

For your love for us, strong and challenging,
      which has called us to risk for you,
asked for the best in us,
      and shown us how to serve,
we give you thanks.

O God, we come to celebrate
      that your Holy Spirit is present deep
            within us,
and at the heart of all life.
      Forgive us when we forget your gift of love
made known to us in Jesus,
      and draw us into your presence.

ALI NEWELL

Lord, what a wonderful feeling it is that I don't have to be someone else ... and they don't have to be me. You have called us each to be ourselves. Help me find the joy today in being me. Amen.

LUCI SWINDOLL

I will sing to the LORD all my life;
I will sing praise to my God as long as I live.
May my meditation be pleasing to him,
as I rejoice in the LORD.

PSALM 104:33–34

Hagar gave this name to the LORD who spoke
to her:"You are the God who sees me,"
for she said,"I have now seen the One who sees me."

GENESIS 16:13

God created man in his own image,
in the image of God he created him;
male and female he created them.

GENESIS 1:27

O LORD, you have searched me
and you know me.
You know when I sit and when I rise;
you perceive my thoughts from afar.
You discern my going out and my lying down;
you are familiar with all my ways.
Before a word is on my tongue
you know it completely, O LORD.
You hem me in—behind and before;
you have laid your hand upon me.
Such knowledge is too wonderful for me,
too lofty for me to attain.

PSALM 139:1–6

Because of you, Lord Jesus, I have the
fullness, the richness, the joyfulness of your
total Deity within my being. Because you
have given me the gift of salvation through
your death on the cross, I have been set free
from the weight of sin. I can enter into new
experiences with ease and gratitude, and give
you praise for these earthly pleasures. Amen.

MARILYN MEBERG

To the saints God has chosen to make
known among the Gentiles the glorious
riches of this mystery, which is
Christ in you, the hope of glory.

COLOSSIANS 1:27

There is now no condemnation for those
who are in Christ Jesus, because through Christ
Jesus the law of the Spirit of life
set me free from the law of sin and death.

ROMANS 8:1–2

God made him who had no sin to be sin for us,
so that in him we might
become the righteousness of God.

2 CORINTHIANS 5:21

God chose us in him before the creation
of the world to be holy and blameless in his
sight. In love he predestined us to be adopted as
his sons through Jesus Christ, in accordance
with his pleasure and will—to the praise of his
glorious grace, which he has freely
given us in the One he loves. In him we have
redemption through his blood, the forgiveness of
sins, in accordance with the riches of God's
grace that he lavished on us with all wisdom
and understanding. And he made known to us
the mystery of his will according to his good
pleasure, which he purposed in Christ.

EPHESIANS 1:4–9

Jesus said, "God so loved the world
that he gave his one and only Son, that whoever
believes in him shall not perish but
have eternal life. For God did not send his
Son into the world to condemn the world,
but to save the world through him."

JOHN 3:16–17

Prayers
FOR *Blessing*
AND *Favor*

Remember your mercies, Lord.

Be gracious to me, O God.

In your love remember me.

Awake, O my soul, awake!

Create a clean heart in me.

Have mercy on me, O God.

You are my strength and my song.

Fill me with joy and gladness.

Open my heart to the service of others.

Make me quick to do your will.

Teach me your paths, O Lord.

O Lord, make haste to help me.

Send me your light and your truth.

Let your peace rest upon me.

Enfold me in your everlasting love.

Keep me on the path of righteousness.

Dwell with us forever, O Lord.

Bless me with your wisdom and counsel.

Forgive me as I forgive others.

Hold me close to your heart, O Lord.

God bless all those that I love.

God bless all those that love me.

God bless all those that love those that I love

And all those that love those that love me.

FROM AN OLD NEW ENGLAND SAMPLER

Have some arrow prayers to pray
during the day.

E. B. PUSEY

"The LORD bless you
and keep you;
the LORD make his face shine upon you
and be gracious to you;
the LORD turn his face toward you
and give you peace."

NUMBERS 6:24–26

From the fullness of his grace
we have all received one blessing after another.

JOHN 1:16

Jesus took the children in his arms,
put his hands on them and blessed them.

MARK 10:16

Praise be to the God and Father of our Lord
Jesus Christ, who has blessed us in the heavenly
realms with every spiritual blessing in Christ.

EPHESIANS 1:3

The same Lord is Lord of all
and richly blesses all who call on him.

ROMANS 10:12

Bless all who worship thee,
From the rising of the sun
Unto the going down of the same.
Of thy goodness, give us;
With thy love, inspire us;
By thy Spirit, guide us;
By thy power, protect us;
In thy mercy, receive us,
Now and always.

FIFTH-CENTURY PRAYER

The everlasting Father bless us with his
blessing everlasting.

THE PRIMER, 1559

Most gracious heavenly Father, creator of heaven
and earth,
I thank you for your blessings—
The deep red cardinal that sits in the branches
of the tree
outside my window
The twinkle in the eye of my granddaughter
when she tickles our big old dog.
The delightful aroma of chocolate chip cookies
just taken from the oven.
The agreeable gift of an unexpected lunch
with an old friend.
The security and warmth of my husband's
playful embrace.
The comfort of knowing someone big and strong
and wise and eternal is looking after me.

A GRATEFUL DAUGHTER

May the Almighty Lord, who bore the reproach of the cross, bless all this family present here. May he who hung on the tree himself lead us to the heavenly kingdom. May he place us at the right hand of the Father, who was made the cause of our peace. Through the mercy of our God, who is blessed and reigns, and governs all things, world without end.

MOZARABIC BREVIARY

"You are worthy, our Lord and God,
to receive glory and honor and power,
for you created all things,
and by your will they were created
and have their being."

REVELATION 4:11

Blessings crown the head of the righteous.

PROVERBS 10:6

Surely, O LORD, you bless the righteous;
you surround them with your favor as
with a shield.

PSALM 5:12

He who has clean hands and a pure heart,
who does not lift up his soul to an idol
or swear by what is false.
He will receive blessing from the LORD
and vindication from God his Savior.

PSALM 24:4–5

God the Father, bless me;
Jesus Christ, defend and keep me;
The power of the Holy Spirit enlighten me
        and sanctify me,
This night and forever.

THE TREASURY OF DEVOTION

The Lord bless you and keep you,
May he show his face to you
        and have mercy on you.
May he turn his countenance to you
        and give you peace.

SAINT FRANCIS OF ASSISI

Go forth into the world in peace;
Be of good courage;
Hold fast that which is good;
Render to no man evil for evil;
Strengthen the fainthearted;
Support the weak;
Help the afflicted;
Honour all men;
Love and serve the Lord,
Rejoicing in the power of the Holy Spirit.
And the blessing of God Almighty, the Father,
the Son,
and the Holy Ghost, be upon you, and remain
with you for ever.

THE PROPOSED PRAYER BOOK

May the love of the Lord Jesus
    draw us to himself.
May the power of the Lord Jesus
    strengthen us in his service.
May the joy of the Lord Jesus
    fill our souls.
May the blessing of God almighty,
    the Father, the Son, and the Holy Spirit,
    be among you and remain with you always.

WILLIAM TEMPLE

Praise the LORD, O my soul,
    and forget not all his benefits—
who forgives all your sins
    and heals all your diseases.

PSALM 103:2-3

The blessing of the Lord rest
*   and remain upon all his people,*
In every land and of every tongue;
The Lord meet in mercy all who seek him;
The Lord comfort all who suffer and mourn;
The Lord hasten his coming,
And give us his people peace by all means.

HANDLEY MOULE

How great is your goodness,
*   which you have stored up*
*   for those who fear you,*
Which you bestow in the sight
*   of men*
*   on those who take refuge in you.*

PSALM 31:19

Love to pray. Feel often during the day the need for prayer, and take trouble to pray. Prayer enlarges the heart until it is capable of containing God's gift of himself. Ask and seek and your heart will grow big enough to receive him.

MOTHER TERESA

Your needs are absolutely guaranteed by the most stringent of warranties, in the plainest, truest words! Knock, seek, ask. But you must read the fine print: "Not as the world giveth, give I unto you."

ANNIE DILLARD

More things are wrought by prayer
Than this world dreams of. Wherefore,
*   let thy voice*
rise like a fountain for me night and day.
For what are men better than sheep or goats
That nourish a blind life within the brain,
If, knowing God, they lift not hands of prayer
Both for themselves and those who
*   call them friend?*
For so the whole round earth is every way
Bound by gold chains about the feet of God.

ALFRED, LORD TENNYSON

SWEET HOUR OF PRAYER

Sweet hour of prayer,
Sweet hour of prayer
    that calls me from a world of care
    and bids me at my Father's throne
    make all my wants and wishes known;
In seasons of distress and grief
    my soul has often found relief
    and oft escaped the tempter's snare
    by thy return,
        Sweet hour of prayer.

Sweet hour of prayer,
Sweet hour of prayer
thy wings shall my petition bear,
to Him whose truth and faithfulness
engage the waiting soul to bless;
And since He bids me seek His face,
believe His words and trust His grace,
I'll cast on Him my every care,
and wait for thee,
Sweet hour of prayer.

WILLIAM B. BRADBURY

SOURCES

www.hymnsite.com

Adventurous Prayer, Women of Faith Study Guide Series, Foreword, Copyright 2003 Thomas Nelson, Inc.

You Can Say that Again, compiled and arranged by R. E. O White. Copyright 1991, p. 245. Used by permission of Zondervan Publishing House.

Prayer: Conversing with God by Rosalind Rinker. Copyright 1970 by Zondervan Publishing House. Used in *NIV Women's Bible 2,* published by Zondervan Publishing House, p. 1067.

God Meets Us Where We Are by Marcia Hollis. Copyright 1989 by Marcia Hollis. Published by Zondervan Publishing House. Used in *NIV Women's Devotional Bible 2* published by Zondervan Publishing House. Used by permission.

Diamonds in the Dust by Joni Eareckson Tada. Copyright 1993 Zondervan Publishing House.

"Small Song," taken from *Polishing the Petoskey Stone* by Luci Shaw. Copyright 1990. Used in *NIV Women's Devotional Bible 2*, published by Zondervan Publishing House. Used by permission of Harold Shaw Publishers.

Lord, You Love to Say Yes, by Ruth Harms Calkin. Copyright 1976. Used by permission of Tyndale House Publishers.

Samuel Johnson (1709–1784)

Thomas à Kempis (1380–1471)

William Cowper (1731–1800)

Ella Wheeler Wilcox (1850–1919)

Prayer from a Mom's Heart by Fern Nichols. Copyright 2003, published by Inspirio, Grand Rapids, MI.

Learning Conversational Prayer, Rosalind Rinker. Copyright 1992, published by The Liturgical Press, Collegeville, Minnesota.

The Book of a Thousand Prayers, compiled by Angela Ashwin. Copyright 2002, published by Zondervan Publishing House.

Overjoyed!, Women of Faith Series. Copyright 1999, published by Zondervan Publishing House.

More Precious Than Silver by Joni Eareckson Tada. Copyright 1993, published by Zondervan Publishing House.

Joy Breaks, Women of Faith Series. Copyright 1997, published by Zondervan Publishing House.

www.sunshine.org/treasure7.htm

Draper's Book of Quotations for the Christian World, Online Quickverse 7.0 version, Edith Draper, Tyndale House Publishers.

Tilling the Soul by Denise George. Copyright 2004, Denise George.

Praying with Women of the Bible by Nancy Kennedy. Copyright 2004, Nancy Kennedy.

Between Two Loves by Nancy Kennedy. Copyright 2003 by Nancy Kennedy.

The New Encyclopedia of Christian Quotations, compiled by Mark Water, copyright 2000 by John Hunt Publishing, Ltd.

We want to hear from you. Please send your comments about this book to us in care of zreview@zondervan.com. Thank you.